All Life Belongs to God

All Life Belongs to God

Erkki Koskenniemi

WIPF & STOCK · Eugene, Oregon

ALL LIFE BELONGS TO GOD

Copyright © 2012. Erkki Koskenniemi All rights reserved. Except for brief quotations in critical publications or reviews, no part of this book may be reproduced in any manner without prior written permission from the publisher. Write: Permissions, Wipf and Stock Publishers, 199 W. 8th Ave., Suite 3, Eugene, OR 97401.

Wipf & Stock
An Imprint of Wipf and Stock Publishers
199 W. 8th Ave., Suite 3
Eugene, OR 97401
www.wipfandstock.com

ISBN 13: 978-1-61097-766-1
Manufactured in the U.S.A.

All scripture quotations, unless otherwise indicated, are taken from the Holy Bible, New International Version®, NIV®. Copyright ©1973, 1978, 1984 by Biblica, Inc.™ Used by permission of Zondervan. All rights reserved worldwide.

Contents

Preface vii
List of Abbreviations ix

1 "You Were Thrown Out..."
   The Gentile Practice 1

2 "For you created my inmost being..."
   Jewish Texts 8

3 "Do Not Kill a Child That Is Already Born..."
   Christian Texts 18

4 Why Did Jews and Christians
   not Expose Children? 35

5 They Did Not Abandon—Or Did They? 53

6 Concluding Remarks 58

   Selected Bibliography 63

Preface

IN RECENT years, quality publications like the *Le Monde Diplomatique* and *The Economist* have reported of shocking statistics in East Asia. Millions upon millions of female babies are missing: if they ever had the right to be born in this world, they were killed immediately after birth. The statistics show that this happens from Armenia to China and Taiwan, among the rich and the poor, and by people from several religions. The reason why parents prefer boys to girls is, following an Indian proverb, they do not want to water their neighbor's garden: A boy will take care of his parents when they get old, but girls go to other families, taking a significant sum of money with them as dowry. This is the reason selective abortions have terminated the life of innumerous baby girls: decided with the help of a cheap scanner, or even killing after birth.

According to the *Le Monde Diplomatique* (July, 2006), 126 boys are born for every 100 girls in Punjab, India, and as many as 138 in Guandong, China. According to *The Economist* (394/2010), no less than thirty to forty million girls will be missing in China alone by 2020, and over one hundred million in the entire Far East. Nobody knows where the "gendercide" (*The Economist*) will lead these societies. We only know that many young men in Asia will seek wives in vain: all the young women of the United States would not be enough to fill the gap in China, and if we look to Asia as a whole, we would have to add the young women of Europe to the number—and it would still be too small.

These alarming statistics show what may happen when people take the right to decide over the life of human beings. However, there was a time when children were abandoned or killed in Europe also. During the classical antiquity, Greeks and Romans exposed or killed babies, both girls and boys. If the parents found that they did not need the newcomer, those societies rarely (if ever) restricted the parent's right to get rid of her or him. Century after century, however, Jewish teachers vehemently opposed the practice and Christian teachers followed in their footsteps immediately after the birth of the new religion. It is interesting to investigate their reasons and arguments for banning the practice. In my opinion, these deserve a careful examination, perhaps more urgently now than in almost two thousand years. They also offer a fresh look on the traditional debate on abortion.

This book does not deal with modern phenomena, but it hopefully gives a new perspective for the debates of today. It is written for people wrestling with the question of the value of human life in its earliest phases; for pastors as well as for teachers and physicians. Those looking for fuller argumentation and discussion with other scholars may read my larger book.[1] I have written the present volume keeping in mind Habakkuk's call for clarity "that he who runs may read it" (2:2). However, I hope that this short volume will show why first Jews and then Christians taught their people to honor the life given by God.

1. Koskenniemi, *The Exposure of Infants*.

List of Abbreviations

Ag. Ap. Josephus, Flavius. *Against. Apion.*

Apoc. Pet. *Apocalypse of Peter.*

Apol. Tertullian. *Apologeticus.*

1 Apol. Justin Martyr. *First Apology.*

ANF *The Ante-Nicene Fathers: Translations of the Writings of the Fathers down to A.D. 325*, Edited by Alexander Robertson and James Donaldson, 10 vols. Grand Rapids: Eerdmans, 1951.

Barn. *Epistle of Barnabas.*

Cels. Origen. *Contra Celsum.*

CCL *Corpus Christianorum, series Latina 1– .* Turnholti: Brepols, 1954.

Did. *Didache.*

Diogn. *The Letter to Diognetus.*

1 En. *First Enoch.*

Ep. Basil. *Epistles.*

FC *The Fathers of the Church 1–* , edited by Hermigild Dressler et al. Washington: The Catholic University of America Press, 1947–.

Gk. Apoc. Ezra *Greek Apocalypse of Ezra.*

Hex. Ambrose. *Hexaemeron libri sex.*

Hexaem. Basil. *Hexaemeron.*

Inst. Lactantius. *Divinae institutiones.*

Leg. Athenagoras. *Legatio pro Christianis.*

Nat. Tertullian. *Ad Nationes.*

NPNF *A Select Library of the Nicene and Post-Nicene Fathers of the Christian Church*, edited by Philip Schaff; 14 + 14 vols. Repr., Grand Rapids: Eerdmans, 1956.

Nupt. Augustine. *Marriage and Concupiscence.*

Oct. Minucius. *Octavius.*

Paed. Clement of Alexandria. *Paedagogus.*

P.Oxy Oxyrhynchus Papyri.

PL *Patrologiae Cursus Completus, Series Latina.* Edited by J.-P. Migne. 217 vols. Paris: Garnier, 1844–1864.

Ps.-Phoc. *Pseudo-Phocylides.*

GCS *Die Griechischen Christlichen Schriftsteller der ersten Jahrhunderte*, edited by Paul Koetschau. Leipzig: Hinrichs'sche Buchhandlung. Berlin: Akademie-Verlag, 1899–.

Sib Or. *The Sibylline Oracles.*

Strom. Clement of Alexandria. *Stromata.*

Symp. Methodius of Olympus. *Symposium.*

t. Makh. Tosefta Makhshirin.

1

"You Were Thrown Out . . ."
The Gentile Practice

Usually, we know the ancient world from through the master's of world literature. Throughout the centuries, scholars have selected only masterpieces to be copied for later generations. Especially in the nineteenth century, they invented another form of record; namely, documents written on small fragments of papyri, which illuminate the daily life of the ancients. These documents included petitions to officials, promissory notes or private letters. They were written and used, perhaps inserted in packaging or inside a human skull. There was no intention to preserve them for scrutiny after two thousand years. One example of such documents is a private letter sent by a man named Ilarion to his wife, who he addressed as "sister," as was typical in correspondence. The document is dated, so that we know it was written on July, 17, 1 BCE It reads as follows:

> Ilarion to Alis his sister, many greetings, and to my dear Berous and Apollinarion. Know that I am still even now at Alexandria; and do not worry if they come back together [?], but I remain at Alexandria. I urge and entreat you to be careful of the child, and if I receive a present

> soon I will send it up to you. If [Apollinarion?] bears offspring, if it is a male let it be, if a female expose it. You told Aphrodisias 'Don't forget me.' How can I forget you? I urge you therefore not to worry. The 29th year of Caesar, Pauni 23.

This beautiful private letter was indeed written two thousand years ago. We here observe the words, "If [Apollinarion?] bears offspring, if it is a male let it be, if a female expose it." The command is clear: an unwanted child should be cast out and left without care. This letter is by no means the only source informing us about the exposure of newborn children. The practice appears in mythology, in drama and in real history.

Graeco-Roman myths mention the rejection and exposure of children. The best-known story tells of a boy whose birth was shadowed by a terrible prophecy. His parents, afraid that it would be fulfilled, had him nailed by his legs to a tree, until shepherds freed him. The boy grew up and was called Oedipus, 'the swollen-footed.' In another tale of children being rejected, Romulus and Remus, the founders or Rome, were nurtured by a she-wolf.

Comedies reflect the daily life of Greeks and Romans more faithfully than do the myths. Plautus and Terence sometimes include exposure in the plots of their comedies: The father ordered the child to be exposed, but the mother could not bring herself to obey; she gave the baby to strangers, years later the child returns and is recognized because of a jewel, or perhaps a protective amulet.

Both mythology and comedy are based on imagination, but the ancient sources often mention cases in which a newborn child was indeed exposed. The social status of the parents varied; they may have been poor or rich. Some philosophers condemned exposure, but we do not know how often it was practiced. Apparently it was common, especially when the child was not wanted or was deformed.

Scholars give sometimes very different definitions of the term 'exposure'. In this book, 'exposure' and 'abandonment' are used as synonyms, and do not mean that a child is given to a monastery, or directly to another family to be fostered, or that a father sells his own offspring. They signify that a newborn baby is left without care during his or her first ten days. This period covers the Greek, Roman and Jewish family feasts customary after a birth. Sometimes the parents may have hoped that someone would take and nurture the child; sometimes they did not care, or even killed the infant, in which case the phenomenon is slightly different. However, both are covered in this book.

The practice among the Greeks and Romans is well known, although scholars rarely agree on the details. It is agreed that financial problems often led to exposure. Sometimes parents simply could not afford to feed their children. Bad years or wars could result in starvation. According to Appian, the year 133 BCE was so terrible that many children were abandoned. However, economic reasons did not necessarily involve lack of food, for even wealthy people would expose their babies because they were not willing to share their property between numerous children. Gentile philosophers would criticize the rich, for being so greedy and miserly as to abandon their children. Very early in Roman history, and again during the reign of Constantine, from the year CE 331, it was legal to sell one's own children, which reduced the number of exposed infants.

Many aspects of the Gentile practice offend a modern reader, and one of them was a culturally accepted reason to abandon a newborn child. The Mediterranean world preferred sons to daughters, and both in drama and in real life it appeared that newborn girls were abandoned because of their gender. Some Greek and Roman writers considered two sons and a daughter an ideal size for a family. The papyri, which contain much information about daily life, attest that families rarely had more than one daughter. The orders of the father were often clear: a girl should be exposed, a son reared. We do not know how many girls were exposed or how many of them survived exposure. However, the practice seems to have been so common that it influenced the structure of the society.

Children born outside of, or before, marriage or by the wrong father may not be welcomed today. In the ancient world, several cases are known in which the child was killed or abandoned for these reasons. Such worries not only troubled young girls from small villages, but the best known scandals even touched the imperial family. Augustus forbade the feeding of a bastard daughter born to his daughter Julia. Claudius believed that the real father of his daughter was a freedman, and solved his problem by leaving the baby without care.

The greatest danger of exposure affected children who were not born healthy. The accounts of how the early Romans treated deformed children are horrifying to a modern reader. Livy reports that a child was born in Frusino that was not clearly male or female. The soothsayers considered the child an omen of disaster, and told people to remove it from Roman territory and drown the child in the sea. Usually, events proceeded smoothly without religious misgivings. It was obvious to Socrates, in Plato's dialogue, that a malformed child is cast out. Seneca, the usually humane philosopher, writes on wrath and says that it must not gain control over a man. This does not, however, mean that he cannot act resolutely and even violently. Monstrous offspring born to animals are killed instantly, but so too are seemingly handicapped children: "Unnatural progeny we destroy, we drown even children who at birth are weak and abnormal. Yet it is not anger, but reason that separates the harmful from the sound."[1]

It was not always easy to distinguish between a healthy and a sickly baby. However, few modern people are able to do make the distinction as exactly as Soranus, the physician, in his handbook. He presents different criteria for the distinction, and says of children not reaching the given standards: "And by conditions contrary to those mentioned, the infant not worth rearing is recognized."[2]

Sometimes, newborn children were abandoned because of bad omens at the moment of their birth. A strange Roman phenomenon, sometimes compared with mass suicide, must be mentioned here. For example, when the beloved Germanicus died, people rebelled against their gods by exposing children. Later, in his astronomical handbook, Firmicus Maternus described the cases in which a child should be reared and those in which it was better to cast it out.

1. Seneca. *De ira*. 1.15.2.
2. Soranus. *Gynecology*, 80.

The simplest reason to abandon a newborn child has not been mentioned. A family could be wealthy, the parents might have no objection to the gender of the child, who was born to a married couple and was healthy. However, it was possible that the parents did not need the child. The child could then be abandoned of killed without further ado. The parents did not need more reason than this to kill or to abandon the child.

The practice of exposure appears in often in the sources, but the sources cannot determine the frequency of the practice. Classical antiquity lasted over a thousand years, and the Graeco-Roman culture was adopted in some measure by many nations from the West to the East. The way of life varied in different times and regions among the numerous nations of the Mediterranean world, which always makes general conclusions dangerous. For example, we should be aware of the following problems with generalizing about the frequency of this practice.

1) Families were small in classical antiquity, but exposure was perhaps not the only reason for this. Child mortality was very high: up to 50 percent of people died before their fifteenth birthday. If we encounter a small family in the sources, was the reason exposure or child mortality or some combination of both?

2) Until recent times, scholars used to amuse their audience by telling anecdotes about ancient contraception and abortion. An amulet may be unable to prevent pregnancy and a crow's egg on the doorstep may not cause a woman who steps over to miscarry; however, our view of the means of contraception in classical

antiquity has drastically changed such that they are now recognized as effective. Exposure was thus not the only method of limiting the size of the family, but to what extent was it necessary in ancient family planning?

3) Scholars have tried to estimate how exposure influences the population, but the problems with estimating are greater than expected. We do not know how many of the exposed infants died, were taken in by childless families, or were reared as slaves. Apparently, when wars did not bring captives to market in peaceful times, the majority of slaves were foundlings.

These points of view illustrate the difficulty of even roughly guessing the number of exposed children. Few scholars dare to offer an estimate of the percentage. However, Polybius, the Greek historian, claimed that the practice emptied Greek cities. At any rate, exposure is mentioned so frequently that it must have been common and known to the ancients from their own experience.

2

"For you created my inmost being..."
Jewish Texts

THE OLD Testament does not contain an explicit ban on the exposure of the newborn children. However, Jewish texts written later than the last books of the Old Testament frequently and severely condemn the practice. It would be easy to explain this by the fifth commandment: it is not allowed to kill a newborn baby or leave her to die. Indeed, several Jewish texts do refer to this commandment. However, this is not the only Old Testament text that influenced early Judaism. Several texts could be involved in the debate, although they do not explicitly mention exposure.

The most important text in the long history may be alien even to people with a profound knowledge of the Scriptures. A legal passage in Exodus describes a situation in which two men quarrel and happen to hurt a pregnant woman. The text is ambiguous. If there is no 'serious injury' (Exod 21:22 NIV; in Hebrew '*ason*), the offender will be fined. If there is a "serious injury" he must give "life for life, eye for eye, tooth for tooth, hand for hand, foot for foot, burn for burn, wound for wound, bruise for bruise" (Exod 21:23 25). First, the passage has troubled exegetes, who do not know whether the mother or the baby is hurt. Secondly, the word '*ason* is problematic: it seems to denote death, and all later texts written in Hebrew or Aramaic interpret it meaning the death of the mother. Perhaps the reason is that a fetus rarely receives a burn and is even less likely to lose a tooth.

Most scholars have solved the problems in the Hebrew text by assuming a development in which different phases of the text have pointed in different directions. However, it was the Greek translation of the Hebrew text, the Septuagint, which became crucial for Western culture. It was made in third century BCE in Greek-speaking Egypt, where Jews did not know enough Hebrew to read their Holy Scriptures. The translation of this passage solves all the problems of the original, but changes the content: it deals with the death not of the mother, but of the child. However, this was not the only change in the text:

> (22) And if two men strive and smite a woman with child, and her child be *born imperfectly formed*, he shall be forced to pay a penalty: as the woman's husband may lay upon him, he shall pay with a valuation. (23) But if it be *perfectly formed* he shall give life for life, eye for eye, tooth for tooth, hand for hand, foot for foot, burning for burning, wound for wound, stripe for stripe (Exod 21:22–23, Brenton LXX)

The translation does not deal with the mother but with the baby; moreover, it distinguishes between a fetus that is "perfectly formed" and one that is not. Apparently, the translation does not refer to malformation but to a sufficient development of the fetus. Perhaps we should observe the argument for the punishment of a murderer in Genesis

9:6: "Whoever sheds the blood of man, by man shall his blood be shed, for in the image of God has God made man." If the fetus is "formed" the offender should be treated as a murderer, but, in the very beginning, the fetus does not have "the image of God."

The Septuagint was used only by Jews who spoke Greek: consequently it does not explain why those using the Hebrew original rejected exposure. At any rate, the passage in the Septuagint greatly influenced the Jewish and later the Christian tradition. However, it was not the only Old Testament text where the unborn child was considered a human being, or where the care of a newborn baby is emphasized.

Some beautiful passages tell about how God created the human in his or her mother's womb. Jeremiah was already chosen to be the prophet to the nations before his birth (Jer. 1:5). In several Psalms, God's work as Creator leads to a touching plea:

> Yet you brought me out of the womb;
> > you made me trust in you
> > even at my mother's breast.
> From birth I was cast upon you;
> > from my mother's womb you have been my
> God (Ps. 22:9–10).

In addition to pleading with God, Psalmists also direct praise and thanksgiving to him. Psalm 139 especially praises God's greatness and wisdom:

> For you created my inmost being;
> > you knit me together in my mother's womb.

> I praise you because I am fearfully and wonderfully made;
> your works are wonderful, I know that full well.
> My frame was not hidden from you
> when I was made in the secret place.
> When I was woven together in the depths of the earth, your eyes saw my unformed body.
> All the days ordained for me were written in your book before one of them came to me (Ps 139:13–16).

God thus loved an individual when she/he was in her/his mother's womb, and consequently after the birth when the baby needed care (Ps. 71: 6). God loves his people like a father or mother: just as a mother cannot "forget a baby at her breast and have no compassion on the child she has borne" God cannot forget his own people (Is. 49:15). Ezekiel's vivid image is a still more relevant: God has picked up Israel as if it were an exposed newborn girl. Simultaneously, this passage offers a very detailed picture of exposure:

> On the day you were born your cord was not cut, nor were you washed with water to make you clean, nor were you rubbed with salt or wrapped in cloths. No one looked on you with pity or had compassion enough to do any of these things for you. Rather, you were thrown out into the open field, for on the day you were born you were despised. Then I passed by and saw you kicking about in your blood, and as you lay there in your blood I said to you: 'Live!' I made you grow like a plant of the field (Ezek 16:4–7).

Thus it is true that the Old Testament does not include a clear ban on exposure, but these passages are nevertheless important to us because they illuminate the ideals of the Old Testament times. The practice was well known, at least to Jews who lived among Gentiles. The picture drawn in Ezekiel was not mere metaphorical for the Jews. These passages were important for and formed the environment in which the Jews reflected on exposure. After all, these texts certainly enabled the devout to apply the fifth commandment on abandonment and, of course, the killing of newborn babies.

Early Judaism produced various, interesting texts, such as the *Sibylline Oracles*. We know of several 'Sibyls' in the Mediterranean world. They were Gentile prophetesses who mediated the messages of gods to Greeks and Romans. Their prophecies were collected in hexameter verse. Jewish people could not help but use the situation: the hexameters of 'Sibyls' were now forged to support Jewish belief and ethics. These verses were indeed addressed to Gentile readers, but surely also to Jews uncertain of their tradition in the pressure among nations. Later, also Christians eagerly used the same method. The hexameters were written by several hands and in different centuries. Two Jewish 'Sibyls' deal with exposure.

The 'third' Sibyl, who apparently lived in Egypt in the second century BCE, wrote rather positively about Gentiles. The writer, through the mouth of the 'Sibyl' gives a very simple instruction: the Gentiles ought to reject idolatry and serve the living God. Moreover, they should avoid adultery and homosexuality, and rear all children born to them, "for the Immortal is angry at whoever commits these sins."[1] This means that exposure is strongly emphasized in these writings: It is one of the very few things mentioned as a distinctive when the Jewish faith is offered to the Gentiles.

The 'Second' Sibyl wrote her or his hexameters after the 'Third', perhaps about the time of Jesus. The attitude toward Gentiles is now totally different. The history of the world is divided into ten generations. Shortly before the end of the world the righteous are distinguished from the ungodly, criterion being as follows: "Again, those who defiled the flesh by licentiousness, or as many as undid the girdle of virginity by secret intercourse, as many as aborted what they carried in the womb, as many as cast forth their offspring unlawfully."[2] This passage tells of one reason God's just judgment will fall on the wicked: they have abandoned their children. We know several similar passages where exposure is frequently mentioned together with abortion. These two are considered unspeakable crimes, which separate the ungodly from the righteous.

First Enoch is a composite work, and it is difficult to date its parts. Apparently, the following passage is written about CE 100, or perhaps even earlier:

> In those days, they [the women] shall become pregnant, but they [the sinners] shall come out and abort their infants and cast them out from their midst; they shall [also] abandon their [other] children, casting their infants out while they are still suckling. They shall neither return

---

1. *Sib. Or.* 3.762–66.
2. Ibid., 2.279–82.

> to them [their babes] nor have compassion upon
> their beloved ones.[3]

Several other Jewish, and subsequently Christian, texts describe the terrible punishments inflicted on sinners after their death. *The Greek Apocalypse of Ezra*, which was written after CE 150, describes such punishments in detail:

> And I saw a woman suspended and four wild beasts were sucking upon her breasts. And the angels said to me: 'She begrudged giving her milk but also cast infants into the rivers.' And I saw terrible darkness and night without stars or moon. There is there neither young nor old, neither brother with brother nor mother with child nor wife with husband. And I wept and said: O, Lord, Lord, have mercy upon the sinners.[4]

Philo of Alexandria belonged to the Jewish elite in his own city, and had received an excellent Greek education in the center of the learned world. Although his tone differs from the texts quoted, he unambiguously condemns exposure in extensive passages and regards it as murder. His main argument is the Septuagint passage quoted above: Because the ending of an unborn life deserves the death sentence, exposure forms a still clearer case. We shall return to Philo's extensive passages later in this book.

Indeed Philo's words clearly represent the views of Jewish teachers in Egypt. Josephus, on the other hand, grew up in Palestine. After the fall of Jerusalem (CE 70), he

---

3. *1 En.* 99.5.
4. *Gk. Apoc. Ezra* 5.1–3.

defended Judaism against anti-Jewish attacks in his work *Against Apion*. He writes as follows:

> The Law orders all the offspring to be brought up, and forbids women either to cause abortion or to make away with the fetus; a woman convicted of this is regarded as an infanticide, because she destroys a soul and diminishes the race.[5]

Because Josephus lived in Palestine and apparently had no Greek education to speak of, he was hardly influenced by the translation in the Septuagint. However, he too considers the rejection of exposure a distinct part of Judaism. It is also important that he refers to legal consequences: a woman who had exposed her child was regarded as infanticide.

It is to be regretted that we only have fragments of the rich Jewish literature written in Jesus' time. The few works extant show how the Jewish teachers taught God's way to their people. We have small fragments of ethical handbooks, which preceded Christian catechisms. Sometimes they speak about the duty to rear all children born alive.

Two Christian texts, the *Epistle of Barnabas* and the *Didache* have preserved a fragment of a lost Jewish work. This ethical handbook contained a ban on the procurement of an abortion and the abandonment of a newborn child. We shall return to this work when dealing with the Christian texts.

Phocylides was a famous Greek poet, and centuries after his death, about the time of Jesus, an anonymous Jew forged verses under his name. Here, as in the case of 'Sibyls,' a Jew pretended to be a Gentile writer. Here, however, the

5. *Ag. Ap.* 2.202.

verses do not deal with the future, but with ethical instruction. Several verses may refer to exposure, but the following words certainly do: "Do not let a woman destroy the unborn babe in her belly, nor after its birth throw it before the dogs and the vultures as prey."[6] We know of several Jewish ethical handbooks. Some of them were reused in Qumran texts, and Josephus too has used one or several of them in *Against Apion* quoted above. It seems that at least many of them ban exposure.

Actually, it is strange that the earliest parts of the Rabbinic literature the Mishna and the Tosefta do not unambiguously ban exposure. Even so, a closer look reveals that they contain passages of significance to us. They show that exposure was forbidden, but sometimes occurred. It is important to note that abortion was allowed only to save the life of the mother. This rule was taken very seriously, and a court judgment was required to proceed with the abortion. Moreover, the rulings exactly defined the stage of birth after which the child must not be killed even to save the life of the mother. It is thus hard to believe that, whoever issued these regulations or followed them, would have allowed the killing or exposure of a newborn child.

Jewish texts often speak of deformed individuals, sometimes of those whose problems were clear immediately after birth. To be true, it is unclear whether parents could diagnose a deformity such as blindness in a child (cf. John 9). However, children born prematurely are sometimes mentioned as well as, more often, infants whose gender was unclear. Rabbinic writings often advise on the infant's treatment as adults. Jesus, too, mentions them (Matt 19:12).

6. Ps.-Phoc. *Sententiae*, 184–85.

Unlike the Greeks and the Romans, Jews allowed these children to live, although their defects were obvious.

Jews zealously protected their people from Gentile blood. Mixed marriages were banned, and, if they occurred, children born in such families belonged to the lowest class of society. But what about children who were foundlings? Did they belong to the chosen people at all? The answers given by rabbis varied. Some considered decisive the population of the city in which the child was found: If the majority were Jews, the foundling was considered a Jew; if it consisted of Gentiles, the child was adjudged a Gentile. However, a saying attributed to Rabbi Judah, the influential teacher, was clearly more severe: "If there was a single Gentile woman or a single maidservant, she is suspected of having abandoned the baby."[7]

R. Judah thus did not consider it possible that a Jewish mother would have abandoned her child. Other teachers seem to have dealt more realistically with the practice: it was banned, but occurred sometimes, however we do not know how often. However, it is important to realize that the religious authorities seem to have done everything to prevent these cases.

Thus numerous Jewish texts deal with exposure. They ban the practice often and severely. These texts have often, unjustly, been neglected. They clearly show how diligently the first Christians emulated their predecessors.

---

7. *T. Makh.* 1.8.

3

"Do Not Kill a Child That Is Already Born..." Christian Texts

CHRISTIANS SOON began to condemn exposure. To be sure, the New Testament does not contain any passages, which deal directly with this theme. However, Eph 6:4 may refer to it: "Fathers, do not exasperate your children; instead, bring them up in the training and instruction of the Lord."

The word used carries a specific meaning to 'bring up,' even 'to rear,' but not 'educate' or the like. In the context where feeding one's own children was not self-evident, a reading which included exposure was fully possible.

Notwithstanding, the condemnation of exposure soon appeared. The earliest texts show how strongly the Christian teachers leaned on their Jewish predecessors.

The *Epistle of Barnabas*, written in Egypt soon after CE 100, describes the two ways open to readers, the way of light and the way of darkness. Exposure is mentioned twice in this context. Believers walking on the way of light received the following instructions: "Do not abort a fetus or kill a child that is already born."[1] In contrast those walking

---

1. *Barn.* 19.5.

on the way of darkness are described as follows: "For they love what is vain, and pursue a reward, showing no mercy to the poor nor toiling for the oppressed; they are prone to slander, not knowing the one who made them; murderers of children and corruptors of what God has fashioned."[2] When the *Diadche*, an important early Christian work, came to light in 1873 scholars soon saw that it also includes advice concerning the two ways. The passages on exposure, too, are very similar: "Do not steal, do not practice magic, do not use enchanted potions, do not abort a fetus or kill a child that is born"[3] And, "For they love what is vain and pursue a reward, showing no mercy to the poor nor toiling for the oppressed nor knowing the one who made them; murderers of children and corruptors of what God has fashioned"[4]

The two early Christian texts are similar in wording, here as in some other parts. A heated discussion soon led to a scholarly consensus. Neither of the works is directly based on the other, but the writers have used a common source. This source, now lost, was a Jewish work, written for internal use and not, as originally assumed, for Jewish mission. The *Letter of Barnabas* contains bitter criticism of the Jews, but thus did not prevent the writer from incorporating a Jewish work, partly verbatim, in his ethical instruction. The *Didache*, written *ca.* 110–120 in Syria or Palestine, reuses the Jewish work as a baptismal catechism: Immediately following the passage on the two ways (chapters 1–6) the writer speaks of baptism, which is performed after the

2. Ibid., 20.2.
3. *Did.* 2.2.
4. Ibid., 5.2.

ethical instruction was completed (7.1). This means that Christianity received the ban on the exposure of newborn babies from the mother religion.

We also know of other Early Christian texts that reject abandonment. We only have two fragments of an *Apocalypse* attributed to Peter. Of these, the Ethiopian, found 1910, is closer to the lost original. The disciples ask the Lord questions about the last things. The answers include the various punishments inflicted on sinners after their death. One sin worthy of severe punishment is abortion, but then follows a passage dealing with our theme:

> Above there, other men and women are standing naked. Their children stand facing them in a delightful place. As the children wail, they groan and call out to God against their parents: 'They neglected us and cursed us, and violating your commandment, they put us to death. They cursed the angel who formed us, and they hung us up. They begrudged us the light which you gave to everybody.' Their mothers' milk runs from their breasts. It thickens and becomes putrid. Meat–eating animals are in it, and they go in and out of it, and they are punished forever, with their husbands. For they abandoned the Law of God, when they killed their children. But the children will be given to the angel Temlakos. Their killers will be punished for ever, because God has required it.[5]

The *Apocalypse of Peter* appears to have been influential, because Clement of Alexandria refers to it and our frag-

---

5. *Apoc. Pet.* 8.5–10 (Buchholz trans.).

ments were written in different languages. The work follows the Jewish tradition, in which the readers were informed in detail about the events after death and the Last Judgment.

The pressure on Christians increased at the end of the second century. The hostility against them was particularly strong among the lowest levels of the society, and sometimes the rage of the mob led to violence and even murder. In this situation, some highly educated Christians wrote apologies addressed especially to the Greek and Roman élite, trying to show that Christians were respectable individuals and good citizens. It is interesting that exposure is often mentioned in this context.

Justin Martyr (martyred *ca.* 163–167) wrote the first apology known to us. His *First Apology* was written about 156 when Polycarp, the old bishop of Smyrna, was burned alive. Christians were accused of eating children at their meetings: the charge was common, of long standing in the Greek world, and had already been brought against Jews. The religious propaganda used it against various groups. Now it was reused against Christians, and this was especially dangerous because it was expressed by Fronto, the strong henchman of Caesar Marcus Aurelius. After some decades, the charges were directed against Punic priests, which led to their crucifixion. The accusations were thus extremely dangerous. Justin chose to counter-attack to defend his fellow Christians.

> But as for us, we have been taught that to expose newly-born children is the part of wicked men; and this we have been taught lest we should do any one an injury, and lest we should sin against God, first, because we see that almost all so ex-

posed (not only the girls, but also the males) are brought up to prostitution. And as the ancients are said to have reared herds of oxen, or goats, or sheep, or grazing horses, so now we see you rear children only for this shameful use; and for this pollution a multitude of females and hermaphrodites, and those who commit unmentionable iniquities, are found in every nation. And you receive the hire of these, and duty and taxes from them, whom you ought to exterminate from your realm. And any one who uses such persons, besides the godless and infamous intercourse, may possibly be having intercourse with his own child, or relative, or brother.[6]

Justin tries by all means to show that Christians formed an ideal group, in which the cruel deeds alleged were impossible. As part of this intention Justin reminds his readers about the exposure of newborn children. Christians rejected the practice—so how could they eat their own children?

Other apologists continued Justin's work. Athenagoras wrote his work between 168 and 170, and addressed it to Caesars Marcus Aurelius and Commodus. Like Justin, Athenagoras too was a cultivated man, who was able to use the manner of educated people when defending Christianity. He also writes on exposure:

Again, what sense does it make to think of us as murderers when we say that women who practice abortion are murderers and will render account to God for abortion? The same man cannot re-

---

6. *1 Apol.* 27.1–3 in *ANF*.

gard that which is in the womb as a living being and for that reason an object of God's concern and then murder it when it has come into the light. Neither can the same man forbid exposing a child that has been born on the grounds that those who do so are murderers and then slay one that has been nourished. On the contrary, we remain the same and unchanging in every way at all times: we are servants of reason and not its masters.[7]

It is easy to see that Athenagoras refutes the same charges as Justin did and with the same arguments. A group that strictly rejects abortion and exposure does not murder its own children. Thus Athenagoras does not give a historically accurate description of Christians, but tries to defend his fellow believers against the rage of the mob by writing to the Caesars and the upper-classes.

An anonymous writer who wrote the letter known as *The Letter to Diognetus* also appeals to the educated elite. This work, written about 176, gives an idealistic picture of Christians and their family life: "Every foreign territory is a homeland for them, every homeland foreign territory. They marry like everyone else and have children, but they do not expose them once they are born. They share their meals but not their partners."[8]

Exposure thus interestingly appears again when Christianity is presented. The Christians live a common family life as respectable individuals; yet, they are faithful to in their marriage vows and do not abandon their chil-

---

7. Athenagoras, *Leg* 35.6 (Schoedel trans.).
8. *Diogn.* 5.5–7 (Ehrman trans.).

dren. The practice is thus very important in the apologetic tradition.

The most fervent of all apologetic writers was Tertullian from North Africa, the first apologist to write in Latin. He wrote two apologies *ca.* 200, and we have every reason to quote them extensively.

> Meanwhile, as I have said, the comparison between us does not fail in another point of view. For if we are infanticides in one sense, you can also hardly be deemed such in any other sense; because, although you are forbidden by the laws to slay newborn infants, it so happens that no laws are evaded with more impunity or greater safety, with the deliberate knowledge of the public, and the suffrages of this entire age. Yet there is no great difference between us, only you do not kill your infants in the way of a sacred rite, nor (as a service) to God. But then you make away with them in a more cruel manner, because you expose them to the cold and hunger, and to wild beasts, or else you get rid of them by the slower death of drowning.[9]

Now the language has changed from Greek to Latin, but the arguments have remained the same. Tertullian, however, is not lenient in his counter-attack. He rejects the charge that Christians ate their children, but ironically recalls that this was precisely what Kronos (Saturnus), the father of all the Greco-Roman gods did, according to the myths. Tertullian returns to the topic in his second apologetic work (*Apologeticus*) written a little later:

9. *Nat.* 1. 15:3–8.

> But in regard to child murder, as it does not matter whether it is committed for a sacred object, or merely at one's self-impulse—although there is a great difference, as we have said, between parricide and homicide—I shall turn to the people generally. How many, think you, of those crowding around and gaping for Christian blood,—how many even of your rulers, notable for their justice to you and for their severe measures against us, may charge their own consciences with the sin of putting their offspring to death? As to any difference in the kind of murder, it is certainly the more cruel way to kill by drowning, or by exposure to cold and hunger and dogs. A mature age has always preferred death by the sword. In our case, murder being once for all forbidden, we may not destroy even the fetus in the womb, while as yet the human being derives blood from other parts of the body for its sustenance. To hinder a birth is merely a speedier man–killing; nor does it matter whether you take away a life that is born, or destroy one that is coming to the birth. That is a man which is going to be one; you have the fruit already in its seed.[10]

As is his wont, Tertullian writes fervently. He here tries to show how Christians lived an ordinary life. However, his writings allow little space for a normal Greco-Roman way of life. Tertullian's attitude to marriage is rather negative, and his strict attitudes finally led him to the radical movement Montanism, in CE 213.

---

10. *Apol.* 9.6–8 *CCSL* 1: 102–3 trans. *ANF.*

Minucius Felix wrote a slightly different apology. Tertullian had been highly educated and was well versed in the Greco-Roman culture, he sought to reject all Gentile education, and his battle cry was: "What has Athens to do with Jerusalem?" Minucius, in contrast, follows Plato's dialogues and lets three close friends discuss Christianity. The first heavily attacks the new religion, but the second defends it. Exposure is, of course, again mentioned in the defense:

> While going in search of promiscuous love adventures, begetting children here and there, and abandoning even those begotten under your own roof, you necessarily must come across your own stock again, and, because of this erratic course, stumble upon your own offspring. Thus, you contrive a tragic plot of incest even when you are not aware of it. We, on the other hand, prove our modesty not by external appearance but by character; so that with a good heart we cling to the bond of one marriage; in our desire for offspring we have only one wife or none at all.[11]

The apology is very traditional: the Christian defends his religion by a counter-attack. Christians should not be considered criminals, but Gentiles should as they abandon their children and moreover, practice incest, albeit unknowingly.

Theologians like Clement of Alexandria wrote their passages on exposure for a Christian readership so that the tone was very different. However, it is clear that he had diligently studied the writings of his predecessors. He refers to the risk of incest when Gentiles abandon their children

---

11. 31.4 Pellegrino, trans. *ANF*.

and then visit brothels.[12] Moreover, he criticizes individuals who take good care of their pets, but do not show mercy to unwanted children and abandon even their own offspring.[13] It is notable that Clement, like Philo, leans on the Mosaic Law (Exod. 22.30; Lev. 22.27), which forbids the removal of the young of an animal before it has suckled for seven days. However, men show no mercy but cast their own children out and thereby forfeit the right to marry at all.[14]

The *Apocalypse of Paul* was apparently written in Egypt *ca*. 250. In this text, "Paul" reports seeing endless tortures inflicted on the ungodly after the Last Judgment. These offenders included also those who had abandoned their own children:

> But I sighed and wept, and I asked and said: Who are these men and women who are strangled in fire and pay their penalties? And he answered me: These are women who defiled the image of God when bringing forth infants out of the womb, and these are the men who lay with them. And their infants addressed the Lord God and the angels who were set over the punishments, saying: Cursed be the hour to our parents, for they defiled the image of God, having the name of God but not observing His precepts: they gave us for food to dogs and to be trodden down of swine: others they threw into the river. But their infants were handed over to the angels of Tartarus who were set over the punishments, that they might lead them to a wide place of mercy: but their

---

12. *Paed.* 3. 3. 21.
13. Ibid., 3, 4.
14. *Strom.* 2.18.192–93.

fathers and mothers were tortured in a perpetual punishment.[15]

The roots of the texts are clearly Jewish, but Christians too had already described the punishments inflicted after death. Exposed children now accuse their cruel elders before God and his angels. Following Jewish belief, specific tasks are attributed to different angels. Some works present the angel as the child's guardian, others say that angels share in God's creative work and some, like the present text, report on the angels who punish sinners after death.

The next texts already show the new elements within Early Christianity. Origen, the learned scholar, wrote an answer to an attack by Celsus (*ca.* 248), which had been published about seventy years earlier. Celsus had, *inter alia*, required that Christians leave this world as soon as possible and they should not beget offspring, because they were not ready to share the common cult and religion. Origen answered that it was not a free choice of Christians to terminate their own life and continues as follows: "But God has allowed us to marry, because all are not fit for the higher, that is, the perfectly pure life; and God would have us to bring up all our children, and not to destroy any of the offspring given us by his providence."[16]

A similar thought appears in Methodius' writings. He wrote his work shortly before the persecutions ended, and entitled it *Symposium*. Like Plato in his famous dialogue, Methodius reports a discussion, but the participants in his dialogue are not men but women and the topic is not love

---

15. *Apoc. Paul*, 40 (James trans.).
16. *Cels.* 8.55 SC 150:300, trans. *ANF.*

(*eros*) but holiness (*hagneia*). Methodius praises virginity and considers marriage only a phase in the history of humankind. Humankind first abandoned marriages between brothers and sisters, then polygamy, and finally Christ preferred virginity to marriage. However, God still creates a child in a mother's womb and therefore it is a grave sin to expose an infant, regardless of whether it is born in or outside marriage. The abandoned children are given to guardian angels and they will one day accuse their own parents before Christ's throne.[17]

The reign of Constantine the Great drastically changed the situation of the Church. It did not remove all difficulties, but the new era produced new problems. The Church now reached broader layers of the society instead of the small groups as in the beginning. This also meant that the question of exposure became urgent both in the East and in the West.

Basil the Great, the most influential teacher of the Eastern Church, was born in a wealthy family with ten children. He was always a man with a strong social responsibility. This is mirrored in his *Hexaemeron*, where he deals with God's work in creation. Basil here presents birds as examples for men. The storks take care of their own parents and the eagles of their offspring. This is not something that all birds do:

> But the *phene*,[18] it is said, will not allow it to perish, she carries it away and brings it up with her young ones. Such are parents who, under the

17. *Symp.* 2. 6. 45.
18. 'Osprey' in the old English version is an arbitrary translation for *phene*, which was perhaps a kind of vulture.

> plea of poverty, expose their children, it is just that they should equally and without preference furnish them with the means of livelihood. Beware of imitating the cruelty of birds with hooked talons. When they see their young are from henceforth capable of encountering the air in their flight, they throw them and pushing them with their wings, and do not take the least care of them.[19]

Every line written by Basil has become important in the Eastern Church. This is especially true concerning the letters that were later designated 'canonical.' One of them advises on how to deal with Christians who had sinned differently. Women who had exposed their children are mentioned here: "A woman who has given birth to a child and abandoned it in the road, if she was able to save it and neglected it, or thought by this means to hide her sin, or was moved by some brutal and inhuman motive, is to be judged as in a case of murder. If, on the other hand, she was unable to provide for it, and the child perish from exposure and want of the necessities of life, the mother is to be pardoned."[20]

Parents who had exposed their children were thus considered as murderers. This meant that the return to the community was very slow. A murderer was treated as follows: "for four years he ought to weep, standing outside the door of the house of prayer . . . after four years he will be admitted among the hearers, and during five years will go out with them. During seven years he will go out with the

19. *Hexaem.* 8.6, PG 29:177–180, transl NPNF.
20. *Ep.* 217.52 PG 32:796, cf. also *Ep.* 199.33 PG 32:728.

kneelers, praying. During four years he will only stand with the faithful, and will not take part in the oblation."

People who had unintentionally killed a man were sentenced for ten years, but exposure was apparently equated with murder. It is interesting to see that Basil, having seen the terrible famine in 369, is the first Father to observe that indeed all parents were able to feed all their children. In such cases it was inappropriate to say that the mother had sinned by casting her baby out.

Like Basil, Gregory of Nyssa and John Chrysostom briefly mention and condemn exposure. However, it was Basil whose words were crucial for the later development of the Eastern Church.

Of the Western Fathers, Lactantius, a man from Northern Africa, dealt with exposure in *Divinae institutiones*. The work was written during and just after the last persecutions, and it was the first *summa* of Christian theology. In the sixth book, Lactantius writes extensively on the topic:

> Therefore let no one imagine that even this is allowed, to strangle newly-born children, which is the greatest impiety; for God breathes into their souls for life, and not for death. But men, that there may be no crime with which they may not pollute their hands, deprive souls as yet innocent and simple of the light which they themselves have not given. Can any one, indeed, expect that they would abstain from the blood of others who do not abstain even from their own? But these are without any controversy wicked and unjust. What are they whom a false piety compels to expose their children? Can they be considered

innocent who expose their own offspring as a prey to dogs, and as far as it depends upon themselves, kill them in a more cruel manner than if they had strangled them? Who can doubt that he is impious who gives occasion for the pity of others? For, although that which he has wished should befall the child—namely, that it should be brought up—he has certainly consigned his own offspring either to servitude or to the brothel? But who does not understand, who is ignorant what things may happen, or are accustomed to happen, in the case of each sex, even through error? For this is shown by the example of Oedipus alone, confused with twofold guilt. It is therefore as wicked to expose, as it is to kill. But truly parricides complain of the scantiness of their means, and allege that they have not enough for bringing up more children; as though, in truth, their means were in the power of those who possess them, or God did not daily make the rich poor, and the poor rich. Wherefore, if any one on account of poverty shall be unable to bring up children, it is better to abstain from the marriage than with wicked hands to mar the work of God.[21]

Divinae Institutiones was addressed to non-Christian readers. According to the sixth book, published shortly before the end of the persecutions, men should show *religio* towards God and *humanitas* towards human beings. The passage quoted above offers an example of this principle. Immediately beforehand Lactantius had condemned the gladiatorial shows and the death sentence. He sums up by

21. Lact. *Inst.* 6.20, transl. NPNF.

describing the value of human life: "Therefore, with regard to this precept of God, there ought to be no exception at all but it is always unlawful to put to death a man, whom God willed to be a sacred animal (*sacrosanctum animal*)."[22]

After the persecution, Constantine called Lactantius to teach his son Crispus (317). This meant that Lactantius was the first Father who could step into the center of power in the new situation.

Basil's *Hexaemeron* made a deep impression on many readers, including to Ambrose of Milan (339–397), who subsequently wrote a work with an identical title. Like Basil, he uses birds as examples for men. They show hospitality and take care of both elders and offspring. Men may act otherwise:

> On the other hand, the females of our species quickly give up nursing even those they love or, if they belong to the wealthier class, disdain the act of nursing. Those who are very poor expose their infants and refuse to lay claim to them when they are discovered. Even the wealthy, in order that their inheritance may not be divided among several, deny in the very womb their own progeny. By the use of parricidal mixtures they snuff out the fruit of their wombs in the genital organs themselves. In this way life is taken away before it is given.[23]

Like Basil, Ambrose deals with different themes, such as how to equitably share the inheritance between the chil-

---

22. Ibid.
23. *Hexaem.* 5.18.58 (FC 14:231).

dren. However, he also condemns the "excessive cruelty when we abandon our own children."[24]

When Augustine (354–430) wrote his works exposure had long been forbidden by earthly laws. This did not mean that the practice was forgotten, and Augustine does not let his own view be in doubt. He often rejects contraception, abortion and exposure in strong terms. The last is regarded as a grave sin, but Augustine does not consider it necessary to give reasons for this view: A "manifest cruelty" is used to cover a "secret sin."[25]

Augustine wrote extensively on family ethics, and just as Basil set the standard in the East, so Augustine was the normative teacher in the medieval West. When both rejected exposure with strong words, the view of the Church was fixed in both the West and the East. By this time, several local synods had already condemned the practice.

---

24. *Hax.* 5.18.61 (*PL* 14:246).
25. *Nupt.* 1.17.

4

Why Did Jews and Christians not Expose Children?

THE PREVIOUS chapters have briefly presented the Jewish and Christian texts that condemn the exposure of children. Now it is time to scrutinize the arguments the writers used to reject the practice. It is astonishing to see how closely the Christian texts follow the Jewish texts.

It is impossible to treat exposure as an isolated issue. It is inextricably linked with wider issues, such as the role of human beings in the world and in the society, the relation between men and women and especially that between God and men. This means that we must patiently start from a distance and discuss related issues in order to properly understand the strongest arguments. Comparison with the current Greco-Roman way of life sheds light on how much the Jewish and Christian ethics differed from it.

Humans Existed Before Birth

The texts quoted above illustrate the old Hebrew view that humans exist before birth, in the mother's womb. This view, present in the Psalms and in Jeremiah (1:5), was taken as a given by Christians. It was, of course, significant that Luke described the meeting of two mothers and two fetuses (Luke 1:44), and that Paul applied Jeremiah's words to himself (Gal 1:15).

The view that humans exist before birth was not unknown in the Greco-Roman world. Strong religious and philosophical movements considered the soul older than the body. Moreover, some philosophers, like the Pythagoreans, believed that humans possessed a soul from conception. Others claimed that the soul developed gradually during the pregnancy, although most assumed that the child received a soul with the first breath. It is conceivable that those views were held in common by Jews and Christians. Tertullian and Augustine eagerly discuss the topic with philosophers, but apparently failed to agree concerning exposure. The Greco-Roman point of view was theoretical, speculating on the moment at which man acquires a soul. Most of them were certain that a newborn child had a soul, but this does not seem to have led to the conclusion that exposure was wrong. According to the Roman law, the fetus was a part of the female body and abortion was not sanctioned. However, it should be observed that even exposure was not forbidden.

Marriage and Children

An important element of the Old Testament world consists in the positive attitude to marriage and the family. The Old Testament reader soon realizes that it was considered shameful to be childless, as the stories of Abraham (Gen 12–20) and Hanna, the mother of Samuel (1 Sam 1–2) attest. Many beautiful Psalms mirror the Hebrew dream: To live among one's own people, surrounded by numerous offspring (Ps 128).

God told the first human beings to "be fruitful and increase in number." (Gen 1:28). Early Judaism did not consider these words a blessing but a commandment, which required to be fulfilled. Consequently, only a few Jewish movements praised virginity. Mostly, it was considered a duty to marry and to procreate. Sometimes, strict rules were laid down: marriage was obligatory, a childless marriage should be terminated, and it was not allowed for a man to marry a woman older than himself. These rulings appear both in Philo's writings and in the oldest rabbinic texts. The Mishnah and the Tosefta also give various opinions concerning how many children were required before God's commandment was fulfilled and the duty to procreate had expired. Sometimes these rules could even regulate how long it was permitted to refrain from sexual intercourse within marriage: a longer period was allowed to sailors and camel drivers than to workers, who lived with their wives daily, but none had permission to neglect God's commandment.

The early Church took a different way from her mother religion. This is partly due to Jesus' words, where virginity was valued in a manner alien to Judaism. Some people were "eunuchs because they were born that way", but others were "eunuchs because of the kingdom of Heaven" (Matt 19:12). Paul, too, esteems virginity (1 Cor 7). Later, new ideas impinged on Christianity. Some of the heretics rejected the entire Old Testament, particularly the positive view of marriage and the family. Already the New Testament criticizes teachers who consider marriage evil and procreation a sin

(1 Tim 4:3). However, these views gained ground in early Church, and were often refuted weakly if at all. It is hard to find any positive role for sexual intercourse even within marriage, for example, in Tertullian's writings. Genesis 1:28, so important in Judaism, was interpreted allegorically, as referring to good thoughts instead of children. Writers who defended marriage might say that virginity was a better alternative, meaning gold, but there was no reason to neglect marriage, meaning silver. These ideas thus differed essentially from early Jewish thought. However, both Jews and Christians tried to protect unborn life.

In the Greek and Roman worlds, sexuality was seldom confined to marriage. However, because the main goal of marriage was to get lawful offspring, it was a strong institution. The decision whether or not to marry was up to the individual, but the society often showed interest in the number of the offspring. In Jesus' time, this meant that the authorities and their advocates, like Polybius and Seneca, sought to boost the population instead of limit it. Augustus, for example, encouraged citizens to marry and to rear more children. Later rulers like Trajan, the Severi, and finally Constantine followed suit as far as possible. To have children was considered a virtue and it was praised. However, this rarely seems to have led to what the rulers had hoped.

Children the Goal of the Sexual Intercourse

The views of Christian teachers thus differed from those of their Jewish colleagues. However, both rejected exposure. For Jews, marriage and procreation were a duty, for many Church fathers a concession on God's part, but neither of them approved of sexual intercourse without the intention to procreate, not even within marriage. In Augustine's words, sexual intercourse without the intention to procreate makes wedlock a brothel and involves a sin, although it is a venial one within marriage. Consequently, both Jewish and Christian tradition overlooked, for example, the exhortation of Proverbs 5 to "rejoice in the wife of your youth."

In the Greco-Roman world, two different views lived side by side. Traditionally, sexuality was not limited to marriage. The goal of marriage was to get lawful offspring, but what could be characterized as love affairs were, as in Classical Athens, heterosexual or homosexual unions outside of marriage. In the Roman world, chastity meant that men left strangers' wives untouched, not that they avoided sexual intercourse with male or female slaves or prostitutes. However, there was also another view on sexuality, growing stronger in late antiquity. Gentile philosophers, who lived at the time of the Church Fathers, often lived according to very severe standards. The discipline preached by the Fathers certainly touched people who considered it wisdom to eat once in two days.

Contraception and Abortion—Yes or No?

Until recently scholars assumed that ancient contraception was too ineffective to be used in family planning, although several methods were mentioned. Some passages recommending magical practices made it easy to laugh at ancient nonsense. However, in 1992 John Riddle made scholars revise their views of ancient methods. He tested the ancient medicaments (especially those recommended by Soranus) with animals and rediscovered the ancient family planning. The medicaments were contraceptive up to 100 percent and also produced an early abortion in most cases. Although the medicaments have not been tested on human beings, most experts no longer doubt their effectiveness, but ask how widely they were known outside of the group of ancient scholars. Apparently, the way did not go from the handbooks to the common people, but the reverse prevailed: the old, popular medicine had invented the methods, which were written down in the medical handbooks. In the classical world, contraception was mostly accepted and abortion was only sometimes morally condemned. Civil laws rarely, if ever, limited such methods before the state became serious concerned about the decreasing population *ca*. CE 200

Jewish sources often mention contraception. Generally, it is typical of the Mishnah and the Tosefta that they often quote the different, contradictory opinions of religious teachers. There were themes that were not subject to discussion, such as monotheism, for example, but others were moot. The duty to be fruitful and increase in number was explicit, but it is unclear when this obligation was fulfilled. After the fulfillment of the duty, some rabbis allowed contraception for women—in their opinion, the commandment was only given to men, while others said that it applied to both men and women. But the views on the number of children required to fulfill the commandment varied.

We only know of negative statements on contraception among Christians, and the reason seems to be the marital ethics described above. If marriage in general was only a concession of God to the weak and children the only goal of sexual intercourse, there was little room for contraception. However, it should be observed that many early writers simultaneously attacked irregular sexual relations and contraception; often it is impossible to know what the writer thought about contraception within marriage. The first writer to condemn contraception seems to be Minucius Felix, although it is not easy to know whether he speaks only of contraception or of abortion as well.[1] Only a few ancient writers were able to distinguish between contraception and abortion, because the medicaments produced an early abortion. However, after Minucius contraception was rejected by, for example, Hippolytus, Hieronymus, John Chrysostom and Augustine.

Jewish sources frequently and harshly condemn abortion. It is frequently listed among sins that were never allowed. Philo, Pseudo-Phocylides, and Josephus briefly condemn abortion. The rabbinic sources allow it when the mother's life is in danger, but always consider the case very serious. The decision to allow embryotomy was made by a court, and the permission might be rescinded at the moment when the head has emerged. Christian teachers agreed on the rejection of abortion, and the first Christian sources dealing with the theme repeat Jewish wordings. Hippolytus and Ambrose condemned abortion later in the *Apocalypse of Peter*. Tertullian and Augustine followed their Jewish predecessors in allowing abortion to save the life of the mother.

The views on contraception and abortion are not directly connected with exposure. However, the comments on them shed considerable light on the sexual ethics, to which the rejection of exposure belongs. People condemn-

1. *Oct.* 30.2.

ing contraception and abortion as evil hardly showed understanding of the abandonment of the children already born. Moreover, the strict limits on embryotomy, which was performed to save the life of the mother, certainly illustrate the view on the life of the child. We shall return to the question later.

An Ideal Community Does not Expose Children

Their religion separated the Jews from many important areas in the Greco-Roman society. To be different often meant to be alien, and it involved hostility and resentment. As stated above, persecutions originated chiefly in rage the lowest levels of the society, and Jews were wont to seek help from enlightened leaders. Jews had a strong tradition to present their own nation as an ideal society that was not hated by reasonable, well-informed individuals. In such writings, as in Philo's *Hypothetica*, preserved in fragments, and Josephus' *Against Apion*, the superior morals of the Jews were emphasized. Both works tell how Jews condemned abortion, and at least Josephus also reports that exposure was rejected.

Christians inherited the problems of the mother religion. A usual element of the ancient religious propaganda was the charge that the opponents practiced human sacrifice. As seen above, Justin states that this dangerous claim was reiterated against Christians. The apologists, who addressed their works to educated individuals, often emphasized that Christians definitely could not slaughter and eat their own children, because they were not even allowed to abandon their offspring. This argument is used by Justin,

Athenagoras, Tertullian, Minucius Felix, and in the *Letter to Diognetus*.

Thus the Christians here too made use of the argument borrowed from the Jews. Apparently, the writers in both traditions considered the argument useful. Although exposure of children was legal in the Greco-Roman world, most people considered it deplorable, a sad necessity. It was thus useful to present Christians as an honorable people who never bowed to necessity. These passages do not describe the real life among Jews and Christians, but the life of an ideal community, which should not be hated and persecuted.

Exposure is Cruel and Against Nature

Philo especially claims that exposure is a cruel practice and, moreover, a practice against nature. Everyone who studies nature sees how irrational creatures take care of their young. Only heartless and cruel individuals can act otherwise and cast out their own offspring, destroying what Nature has formed.

Philo's argument flows from the heart of his religion. In his view, God had created the Universe and given the Mosaic Law: no wonder that the Law is compatible with the world and the world with the Law. It was easy to find contacts with the Greco-Roman wisdom in this perspective: all reasonable thoughts were compatible with God's wisdom or even derived from it. Now it was easy to remind the reader of how, in its mercy, the Mosaic law forbade the slaughter of newborn animals and required that they be allowed to suckle seven days (Lev 22:27). How could men be crueler than animals?

Nature represented a strong authority especially to Stoic philosophers, who saw the need to live in harmony with it. It is thus understandable that Musonius Rufus, the Stoic philosopher, was the strongest critic of exposure, stating explicitly that the practice is against nature. Scholars are tempted to say that Philo had learned his view from the Stoics. Yet Musonius lived after Philo, and we do not know the argument from the earlier philosophers. Moreover, Musonius did not consider the practice always wrong, but told people to raise most of their children. The argument is thus compatible with his desire to boost the number of births in the society. This seems also to have been the main reason why Plutarch said that nature teaches men to respect their offspring.

At any rate, both Jewish and Greco-Roman philosophers told their followers to study nature and to learn from it. Christians were keen to use these arguments. Clement of Alexandria often borrowed from Philo and does so here too. Basil particularly emphasized examples from nature in his *Hexaemeron*. Many actions of birds were—as he believed—models to men when caring for their old and their young. Some birds take over offspring rejected by other birds. In contrast, Basil knows that some birds of prey cast out their own young, and warns Christians not to do so. So, nature offers good and bad examples for Christian life. This model was also followed by Ambrose in the West. His work too was entitled *Hexaemeron* and, like Basil, Ambrose wrote on exposure.

The Destiny of the Exposed Child—Beasts, Slavery or Brothels

Both Jewish and Christian texts often refer to the cruel destiny of the exposed child. It should have sufficed for a horrifying picture to describe how a small human being dies of cold and hunger. However, the writers eagerly presented worse options, beasts, slavery, brothels, and even incest.

The cruel beasts that devoured the children already belonged to the ammunition used by Philo; Jewish writers, such as Pseudo-Phocylides; and Christian, Tertullian and Lactantius, followed suit. The danger was by no means mere imagination. A newborn baby may live several days, although not during the Mediterranean winter, but cold and hunger were hardly fast enough to kill the majority of the exposed children. Various animals still frequent dunghills in the Mediterranean world, and it is hard to believe that in ancient times a single night would pass without their visit. The Old Testament reports that dogs ate Jezebel, left unburied on the street (2 Kgs 9:34–36), but examples from later times are also known. A Rabbi prevented the burial of a heretic on the Sabbath, and next day there was nothing left to be buried. Roman sources, like Seneca and Firmicus Maternus, often mention animals—especially birds and dogs—when speaking about exposure. The arguments used belonged to harsh reality and were not mere exaggeration.

Lactantius stated that parents deliver up their abandoned children into slavery. This may have been a common destiny, and perhaps many parents hoped for it when abandoning their children very early in the morning. Some sources tell of individuals who early in the morning went to collect infants to raise them for slavery. The writer of the Early Christian *Hermas* was such a child. These foundlings are mentioned so frequently that a great many must have been slaves in ancient times. Indeed, during wars, which brought an abundance of prisoners to the market, the price of slaves was so low that there was no reason to raise a newborn child for this purpose. However, the argument was an excellent weapon in the Christian counter-attack, because the owner could do whatever he wanted with the child. The Elder Seneca tells of a cruel man, who used to collect foundlings, maimed them and sent them on the streets to beg for money from the people feeling pity for them. The speakers in Seneca's work—which, fortunately, was fictional— consider the man very cruel but simultaneously say that he acted legally.

Especially Christian writers (Justin, Tertullian, Minucius and Lacantius) often claim that the foundlings grew up to serve in brothels. The argument is harsh, and Justin certainly exaggerates when saying that almost all foundlings, girls as well as boys, had to work as prostitutes. However, numerous writings record that foundlings were raised for brothels, and the worst source is not literary and fictional but archaeological and real. In Ashkelon archaeologists excavated a bathhouse, which was used from the fourth century CE to about the sixth century. The drain contained skeletons of almost one hundred newborn children. Apparently, the bathhouse was a brothel offering a range of services, including prostitutes. Most of the children born to them were thrown into the sewer of the bath immediately after birth. The scholars were able to determine the gender of the children by scrutinizing the DNA. In 19 cases of successful analyses 14 belonged to male and only five to female children. Although usually girls were exposed more often than boys, the number is atypical now. Apparently the girls were spared to succeed their mothers. It is sad to add that pedophilia was not regulated by laws but by the open market in those days. Many Romans had "pet children" for their sexual needs. They were often foundlings and perhaps deformed, pseudo-hermaphrodites or dwarves – greatly appreciated among Romans for this purpose.

Christian teachers eagerly used an argument against pedophilia and brothels in general. Justin was the first author known to us to claim that Gentiles unwillingly practiced incest when they exposed their children and then visited them in brothels, to which they had been brought. Tertullian, Minucius, and Clement of Alexandria repeated this claim. It certainly was the worst kind of propaganda, but it touched the readers and not only because incest was among the worst offences in the eyes of Greeks and Romans. We understand that parents who had cast out their offspring could not help looking at many children begging on the streets. Women gave gifts to them because they feared that by acting otherwise they would fail to help their own children. "Poor woman, if she knows it to be hers, poor woman, if she does not know", says Arellius Fuscus describing the feelings of women gazing at exposed children. Christian apologists targeted their audience to hit where it hurts and it certainly did.

Exposure against Earthly Laws

Tertullian vehemently claimed that exposure of children was illegal. However, it is not easy to understand this claim, because all we know is that it was legal until 374. Tertullian hardly wrote something that everyone of his audience considered nonsense. However, it was typical of him that he sometimes used rather light ammunition. We have several explanations of his words. Some writers claimed that Romulus, the founder of Rome, required the citizens to raise all sons and the first daughter, but the law is clearly unhistorical, mirroring later hopes and ideals. Augustus tried to increase the number of children in the families, and perhaps Tertullian refers indirectly to these ordinances. Apparently some local laws existed, and the Caesars attempted to limit family planning soon after Tertullian. However, we do not know these ordinances in detail, which means that Tertullian's claim remains enigmatic.

Exposure against Heavenly Law

Christians adopted the heaviest argument against exposure from their Jewish predecessors: God's law does not allow the abandonment of children.

As seen above, the Mosaic Law does not include an unambiguous rule on exposure, but Jews were adamant nevertheless, for several reasons. First of all, the word 'Law' did not necessarily mean the written Law among Jews, but sometimes a conventional interpretation thereof; that is, practically the whole Jewish way of life. As seen above, Josephus, for example, may say that the Law requires that all sons be taught to read. The written and the unwritten Law were intimately interwoven.

But the Jews also found several passages in the Torah, which they considered relevant. One of them was the passage quoted above, which in the LXX reading punishes one who kills a fetus as a murderer (Exod. 21:22–25). Philo draws logical consequences: Because it is wrong to kill a fetus, it is certainly also wrong to kill a newborn child or leave it to die. Many Christian teachers, like Tertullian and Augustine, used the same argument to condemn abortion. Moreover, another passage adduced by Philo is Exod. 22:27, which requires believers to show mercy to the offspring of animals. It is easy for Philo to use the same model as above: If people are enjoined to show mercy to the offspring of animals that they must allow to suckle, how can they with impunity be merciless towards newborn children? Clement of Alexandria uses the same argument, which he, of course, had found in Philo's works.

The heaviest argument open to both the Christians and the Jews was the passage, which was seldom explicitly adduced. However, the commandment "You shall not murder" (Exod. 20:13) was the most important Biblical argument against exposure. The long passages in Philo's work *De specialibus legibus* belong to the interpretation of this commandment. The lost Jewish work used in the *Epistle of Barnabas* and the *Didache* quotes this commandment verbatim, when banning abortion and exposure. Lactantius' words belong to a passage, in which he deals with various threats to human life. Moreover, several Jewish and Christian apocalypses observe that individuals who had neglected 'God's Commandment'—obviously the Fifth

Commandment—were punished after death. It is more than probable that the expansion of the Fifth Commandment to cover the exposure of children was an old Jewish "tradition of the elders" (see Mark 7:3), a regulation not included in the Torah, but based on a common interpretation. Christians adopted it as early as we can trace.

The Jewish and Christian point of view here clearly differs from the Greco-Roman thought. In Greece or Rome, rulers did not tell people what to do in their families. *Patria potestas*, the jurisdiction of the father, was an ancient and holy principle in Rome. Everyone in the family stood under his power, and he possessed in theory *ius vitae necisque*, the right to decide who would live and who would die. In Jesus' time this may have been only a principle, although the father who had killed his child was apparently not always punished. But the power was unlimited concerning slaves, and well known to individuals who took a foundling to serve pedophiles in brothels or maimed him to beg for alms on the streets. However, the jurisdiction of the father also covered the life or death of a newborn child. There was no duty to accept or reject a child. Perhaps the best example, although certainly an extreme one, originates from the Greek world. A woman who cohabited with Aristippus, the pupil of Socrates, carried a newborn child to its father and asked what she should do with it. Aristippus told her to cast it out. "But it is from you!" cried the woman. The philosopher spat and said "so is also that but I have no use for it"[2] The formulation may be extreme, but it illustrates the absolute power of parents over their children, so alien to Jewish writers. The society may have hoped for more

2. Stobaeus, 4.24b, 30.

citizens and sought to increase the population, but it was parents and not the authorities who made the decisions concerning individual children.

Several scholars have considered a crucial question, answered differently in the Greco-Roman and Jewish-Christian worlds, whether or not a fetus was regarded as a human being. Actually, this was irrelevant, because philosophers who believed that the fetus has a soul nevertheless allowed abortion. In the contrast, the ancient world distinguished between the biological and the social birth of a human being. Although the terms are modern, they reveal the essential difference. Athenian families used to hold feast called the *amphidromia*. We know very little about it, but it apparently consisted of different elements, of a private celebration, in which women (?) walked around the child, a sacrifice and a subsequent feast. Apparently the traditional function of the banquet was to ensure that the child was strong enough to be accepted into the family; obviously, the parents performed the inspection earlier. Romans had their own feast called the *lustratio*. The biological birth did not guarantee that the child had been accepted into the family. These banquets signified a social birth, and that life had been granted to the newcomer.

The traditional Jewish and Christian view was totally different, and it is best expressed by Lactantius. He condemns exposure and calls a human being *sacrosanctum animal*, 'a holy creature'. This means that Lactantius applies a traditional Roman term to illustrate his view. A tribune of the people was *sacrosanctum*; that is, it was not permitted to anybody to touch him or hinder him in his duties. In a similar manner, a human being is holy and under God's protection. He may not be killed in the amphitheater or executed, but also not abandoned when he is an infant. A Jewish writer may have used different words and allowed a Jewish mother to speak of the light, which she herself had not given to her children.[3] However, the Christian view, distinctly different from the usual Greco-Roman attitude, is directly borrowed from Judaism. Neither the society nor the individuals decide whether or not a child should be raised or killed, but God who has created him. It is not allowed to men to dowse the light that they have not themselves given.

3. *2 Macc* 7.

5

They Did Not Abandon—Or Did They?

SCHOLARS STILL disagree on certain points, especially on the impact of the Jewish and Christian ethical instruction among ordinary people. Individual scholars have long ago emphasized that the reasons for the exposure were not ideological but economic and that religion did not change them at all. According to them, the religious teachers may have preached what they considered right, but the common people did what they considered necessary.

These claims touch the difficult point only too well known to all scholars. The ancient literature mostly represents the views of the higher classes of the society. We have extensive works produced by the elite, but the ordinary people did not write theological treatises. Blind trust in the literature undoubtedly gives a distorted view of the ancient Jewish and Christian reality. However, we have diverse sources, which certainly help us to understand both traditions.

Our Jewish sources originate partly from Palestine and partly from the Diaspora, it may be best to start with the situation in Palestine. Unfortunately, we must also here try to put a jigsaw puzzle together. The only reference to a legal consequence is Josephus' word, according to which a woman who had exposed her baby was considered a murderess. But the Palestinian population included both Jews and Gentiles, and we do not know enough about the legal practices to describe court procedures in detail. Jerusalem was destroyed in CE 70, and this changed everything. The Rabbinic texts compiled one hundred years after the fall of the city do not give detailed rules. However, as stated, they tell what to do when an exposed child is found in a city. A saying attributed to an influential teacher, Rabbi Judah, illustrates the view of the rabbis: if there was a single Gentile woman in the city, it should be assumed that precisely she had abandoned the foundling. We are justified in assuming a strong, social control and juridical consequences of exposure in Palestine. Jewish cemeteries have revealed both very high child mortality and a surprising equality between genders. It would seem that it was not usual to abandon a child, because Jewish texts undoubtedly attest that sons were preferred to daughters, but the archaeological material does not indicate that girls were abandoned more than boys. A second, heavier argument is the appearance of individuals whose defects were obvious at the moment of birth. Pseudo-hermaphrodites, children whose gender was in doubt, or cryptorchid boys were not consistently exposed, because Jewish texts often give rulings concerning them.

The situation in the Diaspora was drastically different from that in Palestine. The Jewish people invariably lived in minority, but the situation varied; in some cities they formed a strong community, but in others they hardly saw other Jews. Usually we know the situation in Egypt best, and this is also true concerning exposure. To be sure, the non-literary sources, mostly the papyri, attest that Jewish families were so small that exposure can justly be assumed; however, the sources never report a single case in which a child was abandoned. Philo apparently addressed his severe words against exposure to his entire audience, which consisted of both Jews and Gentiles. These passages reveal the situation, in which the Jews lived in the Diaspora: the Gentile way of life tempted Jews, and the only means to protect against it was the regular, unambiguous instruction. That is exactly what Philo does in his writings, concerning ethical topics in general and the exposure of children in particular. Both Pseudo-Phocylides' verses and the lost work cited in the *Epistle of Barnabas* and the *Didache* clearly attest the same intention. The Jewish teachers solved the problems in the life in Diaspora by continuous ethical instruction. Of course, this could not prevent an individual from acting like Tiberius Alexander, the relative of Philo: according to Josephus, he left his ancestral way of life. We do not exactly know what that meant, but we understand that the problem touched and still touches all religious minorities in the world.

Concerning the early Christian way of life, our problems are still larger. We know very little about the early Christian family life. We cannot expect that excavations, as in Corinth, will shed light on the practices among the Christians. Christians were a small minority among Gentiles everywhere and did not leave much for archaeologists to excavate. It took centuries before the archaeological sources begin to yield essential help for scholars. The Christian inscriptions start to mention foundlings at the beginning of the fourth century. However, we then know only that a Christian picked up a baby to feed him, but we have no idea who had exposed the child. Secular law criminalized exposure in 374, but the Fathers still continued to refer to foundlings. The excavations in the bathhouse at Ashkelon attest that the law by no means protected the life of the newborn.

Children were thus abandoned, but how often did Christian parents expose them? The earliest sources written after the New Testament already make clear that Christian teachers tried to prevent the practice by moral instruction. This instruction is reiterated so often after the *Letter of Barnabas* and the *Didache* that it was undoubtedly a feature of Christian moral education. Simultaneously, of course, it reveals that the danger was considered real. No one repeats ethical rules again and again if he is satisfied with the state of things.

The Christians in the West today live in a world in which every individual increasingly makes her or his ethical decisions independently. Christian Churches may give their moral instruction, but the birth rate is so low in the Roman Catholic countries that contraception is commonly used, and abortions are frequent in the nominally Lutheran Northern Europe as well as in the mainly Orthodox countries. In this situation, people are tempted to project their own world onto the life of ancient Jews and Christians. This is hazardous, however, because the ancients often listened to their teachers, although the people of today perhaps do not. Palestinian Jewish towns were not like modern Western cities in which individuals freely decided on their way of life, but practiced strong social control. The Fathers too indeed influenced the behavior of their audience. A single, severe, sermon by Augustine was needed to end a traditional banquet, which had led to violent quarrels.

Both Jewish and Christian teachers strongly opposed exposure, and it certainly had an impact and reduced the abandonment of children. However, there is no reason for idealism. Babies were undoubtedly cast out among Jews and Christians. This was the reason why the religious teachers were never tired of repeating that it is a serious sin against God.

6

Concluding Remarks

THE INVESTIGATION of the texts dealing with exposure is a very moving, saddening task. The material includes horrifying details, which have much to teach a modern reader. Simultaneously, both the writer and the reader should remember that we are concerned with a very sensitive subject.

The first important lesson has been to realize how closely the first Christians followed Jewish writers. Although neither the Old nor the New Testament include an unambiguous ban on exposure, the Christians had no difficulty in perceiving the Jewish tradition. Jewish teachers had connected exposure with the fifth commandment, and the Christians followed in their footsteps. The other arguments were mostly derived from the Jewish tradition, with one significant exception. Unlike the mother religion, Christian teachers preferred virginity to marriage and family life. This ideal was not taken from the New Testament. When the Church abandoned the Old Testament's positive attitude to marriage and sexuality she did not change for the better.

However, by and large, the Christian moral instruction was compatible with the Jewish and clearly differed from the Greco-Roman way of life. Scrutiny of the texts dealing with exposure indicates the crucial value of a human life. The Greco-Roman world divided life into two areas, one regulated by the society and the other by the individual, here the father of the child. Whether the father decided to raise or to abandon the child the role of the society was not to make objections, but his right was acknowledged, even against the intention of the common good. This right was not acknowledged among Jews or Christians, for whom newborn human being was not subject to the absolute power of his/her parents, but stood under the protection of God. It was not allowed to dowse the light given by God. Because of God's creation, a human being is a *sacrosanctum animal*, a holy creature, and he may not be injured, hurt or killed.

This Jewish and Christian attitude has formed the European concept of the value of human life. It is astonishing to see how Jews and Christians once defended the life of the exposed child with same arguments that are used today to save the unborn. Simultaneously, the strongest argument for 'pro choice' is the right of the individual to make decisions concerning his/her own life. In our time, this means focusing not on the role of the father but on the mother and her right to decide concerning her own body. However, the question has principally remained the same: should issues be decided by the society and the law or by an individual? The ancient world attributed the right to the individual yielded. This is exactly the way our modern society has taken. 'Pro choice' means the right of an individual to choose, not the society. From the Jewish and Christian point of view, the third, most important actor in the process has been totally forgotten; namely, God the Creator.

A human being, including one newborn, even unborn, is a masterpiece of God, and no one has right to destroy it.

Apparently it took time before the Church offered a credible alternative for parents unable or unwilling to feed their children. The earliest documents only require that children must be raised and deprives individuals who are barren of the moral right to marry. In epitaphs from the fourth century, however, individual Christians proudly record that they rescued foundlings and raised them. The Cappadocian Fathers, especially Saint Basil the Great, emphasized Christian responsibility and led the way by their own initiative and immense contributions. They also showed understanding to parents, who were unable to feed their children but had to abandon or sell some of them. According to Augustine, Christian virgins rescued picked foundlings. Apparently, monasteries at first provided an alternative for parents who did not know what to do.

But what are the alternatives our society and Churches offer to women who feel they must resort to abortion? Some Fathers considered it enough to depict the evil and bring accusations, but did Tertullian, for example, have other intentions than to present the evidence of the sins of the world? I should like to say that this path was taken to the end before the great persecutions ceased, but was not.

In Jesus' time Greeks and Romans had their own way of life, which continuously threatened Jewish and later Christian ethics. Minorities were at risk of adopting standards of the majority, then as well as now. The only method of defending their tradition was continuous ethical instruction. Apparently, all the Christian Churches in the West are moving towards an analogous situation. The new laws enabled by societies rarely support the Christian way of life. The only method left is that which was open to Jews and Christians: continuous, active, ethical instruction, which reaches the believers and actively seeks to enlighten outsiders, too.

Selected Bibliography

Athenagoras, *Legatio and De Resurrectione*. Edited and translated by William R. Schoedel. Oxford: Clarendon Press, 1972.

Boswell, John. *The Kindness of Strangers: The Abandonment of Children in Western Europe from Late Antiquity to the Renaissance*. New York: Pantheon Books, 1988.

Buchholz, Dennis D. *Your Eyes Will Be Opened: A Study in the Greek (Ethiopic) Apocalypse of Peter*. SBL Dissertation Series 97. Atlanta, GA: Scholars Press, 1988.

Cameron, Averil, "The Exposure of Children and Greek Ethics." *The Classical Review.* 46:3 (1932) 105–14.

Corbier, Mireille, "Child Exposure and Abandonment," in *Childhood, Class and Kin in the Roman World*, edited by Suzane Dixon, 52–73. London: Routledge, 2001.

Eyben, Emiel, "Family Planning in Graeco-Roman Antiquity." *Ancient Society* 11–12 (1980–81) 5–82.

Gorman, Michael J., *Abortion and the Early Church: Christian, Jewish and Pagan Attitudes in the Greco-Roman World*. Eugene OR: Wipf & Stock Publishers, 1998.

Gray, Patrick, "Abortion, Infanticide and the Social Rhetoric of the Apocalypse of Peter." *Journal of Early Christian Studies* 9:3 (2001) 313–37.

Harris, William V., "Child-Exposure in the Roman Empire." *The Journal of Roman Studies* 84 (1994) 1–22.

Ilan Tal. *Jewish Women in Greco-Roman Palestine: An Inquiry into Image and Status*. Texte und Studien zum Antiken Judentum 44. Tübingen: Mohr, 1995.

———. *Integrating Women in the Second Temple History*. Texte und Studien zum Antiken Judentum 76. Tübingen: Mohr, 1999.

Kapparis, Konstantinos, *Abortion in the Ancient World*. London: Duckworth, 2002.

Koskenniemi, Erkki, *The Exposure of Infants among Jews and Christians in Antiquity*. The Social World of Biblical Antiquity, Second Series, 4. Sheffield: Sheffield Phoenix Press 2009.

———. "Right to life and Jewish-Christian Ethics in the Roman World: A Case Study of the Fighting Men and the Unhappy Birth." In *Encounters of the Children of Abraham from Ancient to Modern Times*, edited by Antti Laato and Pekka Lindqvist, 47–73. Brill 2010.

Motomura, R., "The Practice of Exposing Infants and its Effects on the Development of Slavery in the Ancient World." In *Forms of Control and Subordination in Antiquity*, edited by Tōru Yuge and Masaoki Doi, 410–415. Leiden: Brill, 1988.

Noonan, John T., Jr. *Contraception: A History of its Treatment by the Catholic Theologians and Canonists*. Cambridge: Belknap Press of Harvard University Press, 1965.

Pomeroy, Sarah B., *Goddesses, Whores, Wives and Slaves: Women in Classical Antiquity*. New York: Schocken, 1975.

———. "Infanticide in Hellenistic Greece." In *Images of Women in Antiquity*, edited by Averil Cameron and Amélie Kuhrt, 207–22. London: Helm, 1983.

Reinhartz, Adele. "Philo on Infanticide." *The Studia Philonica Annual*. 4 (1992) 42–58.

Riddle, John M. *Contraception and Abortion from the Ancient World to the Renaissance*. Cambridge: Harvard University Press, 1992.

Schwartz, Daniel R. "Did the Jews Practice Infant Exposure and Infanticide in Antiquity?" *The Studia Philonica Annual*. 16 (2004) 61–95.

Soranus. *Gynecology*. Translated by Owsie Temkin. Baltimore: Johns Hopkins University Press. 1956.

www.ingramcontent.com/pod-product-compliance
Lightning Source LLC
Chambersburg PA
CBHW051705090426
42736CB00013B/2542